# Single but not alone

# Single but not alone

## MEDITATIONS FOR CHRISTIAN WOMEN

Jane Graver

Publishing House
St. Louis

3558 South Jefferson Avenue, St. Louis, MO 63118

Manufactured in the United States of America

---

Library of Congress Cataloging in Publication Data

Graver, Jane, 1931-
Single but not alone.

1. Single women — Prayer-books and devotions — English. I. Title.
BV4596.S5G73 1983 242'.6432 82-14425
ISBN 0-570-03880-4

---

1 2 3 4 5 6 7 8 9 10 CB 92 91 90 89 88 87 86 85 84 83

# CONTENTS

# Foreword

The single woman of today has come a long way from yesterday's stereotype of the faded old maid. In many cases she has consciously chosen not to marry. If she has had singlehood thrust upon her by the circumstances of her life, she finds that it is indeed possible to build a good life when one is alone.

Liberation, however, is not without cost. Ready or not, today's single Christian must manage her own affairs, build human relationships in a world designed for couples, and defend values that many will label old-fashioned. How does she cope with society's multiple expectations? with the well-meant meddling of her friends and family? with loneliness? with intimacy? What does the Gospel have to say to her?

Jane Graver addresses with honesty and insight the problems and successes in the life of a single Christian. SINGLE BUT NOT ALONE offers support for the woman who strives to understand her own feelings of achievement, vulnerability, or anger. . . who wants to take whatever action is possible and then lay the rest in God's hands. . . who rejoices in the opportunities and joys of a single life as lived in the presence of God.

The Publisher

# 1 Lonely

He (Jesus) would go away to lonely places, where He prayed. Luke 5:16 TEV

Even now sometimes, a sharp wave of longing sweeps over me — for a place where there is firelight and closeness and laughter. It's like looking through a lighted window from the bleak isolation of a deserted street. Although I know it's irrational, I feel forever cut off from the caring people inside.

At least I can talk to You about it now, Jesus. For a long time I couldn't even admit my loneliness to myself. To me, to be *lonely* meant rejection — failure — that I was too uninteresting to attract companions. Worse, my false cheeriness drove potential friends away. I denied people the chance to know me as I really am.

Your life, Jesus, helps me understand that loneliness is a universal feeling — one that You, too, have experienced. I can use my lonely days as You did Your time alone — as an opportunity for renewal. I can use hours of solitude to pursue my own interests, to take stock of where I am and where I am going, to make decisions, and to pray. I can enjoy my own company, invite myself to go on a long walk, or make a visit to the art museum or the library. I know now that it is OK to be alone.

Oh, I don't have it all together yet, Jesus, but I'm proud of the progress I have made. These days I push myself to make specific plans for entertainment and mental stimulation, to give myself the pleasure of anticipation. Would you believe that I had never used Your gift of freedom, Lord? never asked myself what my real interests are? never investigated the opportunities for pursuing those interests in this city? I was so afraid of being bored by others, that I ended up boring myself — so careful to avoid an uncomfortable evening that I never tried anything new. Thank You, Lord, for giving me the courage to take risks. I'll never really be a joiner — but it's been fun learning folk dances, studying the Bible, and playing softball and backgammon — and I've met some congenial people along the way.

Another gift that I have learned to use is the pleasantly comfortable home You have given me. After years of being a perpetual guest, the hostess role felt strange and uncomfortable. Remember how I worried about what to serve, whom to invite, and what to plan for entertainment? Thank You, Lord, for showing me that simple food and a warm welcome are an unbeatable combination.

Most of all, Lord Jesus, I thank You for becoming human like me. Thank You for understanding me, for caring about me, and for giving me the ability to change. Because You accept me as I am, I can accept myself — and show the real me to others. Your sacrificial love has turned the emptiness in my life into space — space for growing and becoming.

# 2 Independence

Don't worry about anything, but in all your prayers ask God for what you need, always asking Him with a thankful heart. And God's peace, which is far beyond . . . understanding, will keep your hearts and minds safe in union with Christ Jesus. Philippians 4:6-7 TEV

I can do it! I can take care of myself — be responsible for my own life. I know now who I am — Lord, I am a capable person! I can deal with a leaky faucet, a dead battery, the fine print on an insurance policy. Oh, I am not supercompetent in all these areas — but who is? Nowadays I have enough confidence to ask someone to lend a hand — without giving off "poor helpless woman" signals. After all, sometimes the helping hands are mine; sometimes others turn to me for advice and care.

Thank You, Father, for this victory. You know it hasn't been easy to break a lifelong pattern of dependency. Up to now, there has always been somebody there to take care of me. Up to now, I looked to someone else for security and happiness.

Part of me wants to go back to that comfort and safety, Lord. I puzzle over my budget, my savings plan, and my protection against financial and medical emergencies. What if I make a mistake? My family worries because I drive my own car in bad weather and late at night. What if something happens? My friends say I will become self-centered because I make my own choices, and live by my own rules. But if I don't look after myself, who will?

So the risks are there, Father. Independence is not free, but it is worth the price. Walk with me, Lord, as I learn to walk alone. Thank You for meeting my past, present and future needs. Continue to teach me to be dependent wholly on You.

When I remember to center my thoughts on You, O God, tension and worry melt away. What terrors can possibly threaten me? I have been promised a mind "safe in union with Christ Jesus!" Your miraculous peace enfolds me. I rest in You.

# 3 Christmas Day

> Mary said,
> "My heart praises the Lord;
> my soul is glad because of God my Savior,
> for He has remembered me, His lowly servant!
> From now on all people will call me happy,
> because of the great things the Mighty God has done for me."
> Luke 1:46-49 TEV

I'm ashamed, Lord — ashamed to admit, even to myself, that I am dreading Your birthday,

Where did the magic go? I remember surprises and candlelight and singing and hotly contested games and wonderful smells from the kitchen. The family was intact then. I saw the future through a glamorous TV-inspired mist — a sadly distorted picture of the real world.

That was a long time ago. Lately it's been Christmas with my sister and her family. Lord, I do love them, and I know they love me — but I don't want to celebrate Your day with them. Not this year.

So what are my options? How can I recapture the joy I used to know at Christmas — or at least dull the pain? Well, I could volunteer for the day at a hospital or nursing home, and give a regular worker a chance to spend Christmas at home. Or what about a potluck dinner party that includes every single I know who doesn't have plans? They don't want to be alone, either — so what do I have to lose?

Here's a radical idea. I could spend Christmas Day at home, alone with You. It could be a day to give myself surprises, a day to prepare a gourmet dinner or read that book I've never had time for. It could be a time of special closeness to You — a time to remember how You, Mighty God, have touched my life — a time to consider, regroup, and invite Your Spirit's guidance as I plan my future path.

When I remember Christmas as it used to be, remind me to enjoy my memories but not idealize them so much that no present reality can possibly compete. Help me to balance tradition with change, respect family ties but also meet my own needs, and above all hold fast to the meaning Your birth has for me.

Thank You, Lord, for the part of Christmas that will never lose its magic — the moment when I realize fully that the Sunrise has indeed come, that darkness and death are forever vanquished, and that You, our merciful and tender God, have taken the world into Your arms. Let me praise You with my worship and my life on this Your blessed birthday.

# 4 Guest at His Supper

As they were eating, Jesus took bread, and blessed, and broke it, and gave it to the disciples and said, "Take, eat; this is My body." And He took a cup, and when He had given thanks He gave it to them, saying, "Drink of it, all of you; for this is My blood of the covenant, which is poured out for many for the forgiveness of sins." Matthew 26:26-28 RSV

Here I am again, Lord — unready — incomplete — unworthy to be one with You.

You know all the ways I have failed You this week. You see my self-centeredness — the empty busyness that shuts You out — the preoccupation with everything but the "one thing needful." You recognize the laziness that tempts me to misuse my freedom — to evade all commitments and all responsibilities. You are aware of my lack of trust, my shallowness, and my pride.

Yet You reach out to me in welcome, ready to renew and forgive.

I stand before You with empty hands. Fill me with the gift of Your presence.

# 5 Parents

The Lord says,
"Do not cling to events of the past
or dwell on what happened long ago.
Watch out for the new thing I am going to do.
It is happening already — you can see it now!"
Isaiah 43:18-19a TEV

I'm trapped, Lord, caught in a web of dependence, resentment, guilt, and anger. Again and again, I find myself reworking the past, regretting the missed opportunities, the unwise choices, and the years that now seem wasted. Why have I allowed others to make decisions for me? Why do my parents still try to control my life? Why must they load me with their advice, their worry, and their disappointment?

Lord, it's a vicious circle! They are disappointed because I have not married and provided them with grandchildren. So I feel guilty about causing them pain — and angry at the same time. If my growth had not been stunted by all that well-meant interference, I would be a more independent person by now. Perhaps I would even be married, who knows? If they were not dependent on me in so many ways, I would be free to look for a different job, live far away from here, and turn my way of living around. If only my parents were different, I would be different, too.

Perhaps it's not too late. In spite of the self-pity

that engulfs me right now, I do see Your hand in my life. Surely You are working through the people and events that have pushed me to change and grow. Led by Your love, I am slowly learning to see myself as You see me. I am a lovable, capable person!

Now that I accept myself, Lord, I can accept other flawed human beings as they are. As the gift of Your forgiveness in Christ becomes more real to me, I can forgive those who shaped my yesterdays. I can stop dwelling on what might have been.

Loving Father, show me how to break free from the destructive patterns of the past. Strengthen me as I struggle to take responsibility for my own life. Fill me with love, tact, and firmness of purpose as I talk with my parents. Let me listen to their ideas, respect their feelings, and still be true to my own convictions.

Thank You, Lord, for the mysterious power You have released in my life. I don't understand why I have Your infinite, unconditional love — or why You encourage me to call You "Father." With Your arms around me, I can let go of the past. I can admit that my power over the future is real but limited. All I can count on is now a time to work and ponder and pray and watch for the "new thing" You have promised.

What new thing? A life-changing event? New ideas, new insight, new energy? Strength to endure? Even though I may not recognize Your gift at the time I receive it, Lord, I trust in Your promise and rejoice in Your love.

# 6 Search for Myself

"What about you?" He [Jesus] asked them. "Who do you say I am?"

Simon Peter answered, "You are the Messiah, the Son of the living God." Matthew 16:15-16 TEV

Each one, as a good manager of God's different gifts, must use for the good of others the special gift he has received from God. 1 Peter 4:10 TEV

Never again. Never again will I pretend to be what I am not. Never again will I try to remodel my personality to fit the "ideal woman" specifications of the boss — or the current man — whom I am trying to impress. The new *I* will be totally up front with everyone. My new motto is "What you see is what you get."

Heavenly Father, I confess that I have not been a good manager of Your gifts to me; I'm not even totally clear on what they are. Up to now, I've been busy trying to please everyone, struggling to make myself into what they want me to be.

Lord God, You never intended me to be an interchangeable part. What unique talents have You created in me? What do I have to give Your world? How can I find my real self, stripped of all those layers of self-deception and self-hatred? How can I develop the potential that You see in me?

When I do learn to know and appreciate myself, Father, use my new self-love to turn me outward — free to love others as I do myself. Teach me to care *more* about others rather than care *less* about me. Give me perspective enough to see that one rejection is not the end of the world, patience enough to wait for friends who will prize what I have to offer, and sensitivity enough to truly communicate with others.

Above all, let me respond to the question of Your Son: "Who do you say I am?" Unless I know that He is my Savior, all other search for self-discovery is pointless. It is only under His lordship that my life has any meaning.

Using the strength supplied by Your indwelling Spirit, guide me, Lord, as I set my goals. Fill me with power to meet my own expectations — that I may never again allow others to define "success" for me.

Even with Your Spirit within me, I can still make mistakes; my future is still uncertain. But without You I can do nothing at all. Therefore — let my discovery of self be for Your glory, for any gifts I may have were put there by You. Accept my life as an outpouring of praise, through Christ Jesus, my Lord.

# 7 The Friendship

Since you are God's dear children, you must try to be like Him. Your life must be controlled by love, just as Christ loved us and gave His life for us as a sweet-smelling offering and sacrifice that pleases God. Ephesians 5:1-2 TEV

Help me not to goof this up, Lord Jesus. Restrain me from pushing too hard and from spoiling this fragile new relationship by coming on too strong. I want his friendship. But if he thinks I'm anxious for more, he's likely to back away.

So far it's been pleasantly casual — we run into each other at lunchtime or after work. On the spur of the moment, we spend an hour or so over a snack and a cup of coffee, talking about all sorts of things. All very unplanned — except that lately I eat at his favorite restaurant much oftener than I used to.

I value my women friends, Jesus — but these encounters have added new zest to my life. Our conversations are a stimulating exploration of two quite different points of view. That's all I want — at least for now. Surely a man and woman can have an undemanding friendship without romantic overtones — can't we?

What happens next, Lord? I'd really like to know him better. Should I enjoy the occasional hour we share and let it go at that? Or should I "just happen to have two theater tickets" sometime? Or would it be better to come up with a plausible reason for asking him to my apartment? I could use advice from somone who knows about stereo systems — or income averaging — or drawers that stick.

Wait a minute. If I decide to invite him over — for dinner, for instance — do I need any reason other than that I enjoy his company? Real friendship doesn't mix with playing games. If I accept the limitations of this relationship in my own mind, surely I can offer casual hospitality without making him feel hunted by a man-hungry female. Surely we can bring any cause for tension out into the open and talk it through. It won't be easy; there's always the risk that he will misinterpret what I say or do.

Maybe You thought the risk was worth taking, Jesus. Women were included among Your close friends. You felt free to drop in on them unexpectedly and made it plain You were more interested in good talk than in a fancy dinner.

Lead me, Lord, as I try to follow Your example, as I offer friendship with no strings. Let me always be truthful and loving — accepting the risk of being hurt. Help me find a tactful balance between embarrassing frankness and artful trickery. Make me sensitive to his feelings — to his apparent fear of entangling ties. Protect me from the trap of self-deception, that I may neither use another person in the name of love nor allow myself to be similarly exploited.

From this day on, let my life — and my relationships — be completely controlled by Your love.

# 8 Envy

Whoever listens to the Word but does not put it into practice is like a man who looks in a mirror and sees himself as he is. He takes a good look at himself and then goes away and at once forgets what he looks like. But whoever looks closely into the perfect law that sets people free, who keeps on paying attention to it and does not simply listen and then forget it, but puts it into practice — that person will be blessed by God in what he does.

James 1:23-25 TEV

She looks great in anything, Lord. Hair always just right, clothes never wrinkled, a perfect size 9. She's frighteningly well-organized, witty, articulate. On the other hand, I cringe inside when I catch an unexpected look at myself in a mirror. When I'm with people I don't know very well, I'm timidly silent — or I babble nervously about nothing. If only I had her looks, her assurance! You know that I wouldn't use those gifts with the coldblooded selfishness I see in *her*.

Forgive my envious judging, God. To You, both of us are wonderful, unique persons. You have made us so. When I appreciate her strengths — and my own — I honor You, our Creator.

Lord, hold up the mirror of Your law before me; help me see myself through Your loving but penetrating eyes. Let an honest self-appraisal enable me to rejoice in my strengths — and make specific plans for improvement where I am weak.

Thank You, Father, for the special qualities You

have given me, the traits that make me both lovable and capable. Forgive me for pretending that these rich gifts are worthless — of no account. Show me how to give myself realistic encouragement and how to allow myself the same kindness, consideration, and forgiveness that I would unhesitatingly offer a friend. Forgive my stupid inability to accept a compliment without implying that the giver is either mistaken or insincere. Thank You for people who appreciate me and who help free me to become my best self.

Even so, Lord, I can hardly bear to look clearly at myself. I see so many faults, so many things I'd like to change. When I look at Your perfect law of love, I must admit, all over again, that I am totally unable to follow You on my own.

Once I acknowledge that, I can move out of darkness. Let Your glorious light turn me from self-absorbed misery to an adventurous search, to an eager study of Your Word and Your will for my life. Imperfect though I am, allow me to share in Your rich harvest of goodness, righteousness, and truth.

# 9 One, Please

Not that I complain of want; for I have learned, in whatever state I am, to be content. I know how to be abased, and I know how to abound; in any and all circumstances I have learned the secret of facing plenty and hunger, abundance and want. I can do all things in Him who strengthens me.

Philippians 4:11-13 RSV

"One, please." Thank You, Lord, for helping me say that less apologetically than I used to. You have given me the courage to walk confidently alone into a room, to ask boldly for a good table in a restaurant. No longer do I feel like an outcast, just because I am by myself.

I can go out alone now, Lord, to concerts, parties, and church suppers — and enjoy them. I even travel alone, balancing sociability with caution, adventure with safety. Away from familiar places, I'm more willing to risk refusal, more ready to suggest dinner or sightseeing with new acquaintances, more open to new experiences and new friends of 9 to 90. And if someone assumes that every unescorted woman is looking for a pickup, that's his problem, not mine.

Lord, You have taught me to look for the good in each set of circumstances. When I am with people I care about, I rejoice in their companionship. Alone, I revel in my freedom to respond to the friendliness of others and make impromptu plans with them; I appreciate being able to follow my own moods and my own interests.

Sure, it's lonely sometimes. My dinnertime book is no substitute for a friend's face across the table. The play loses a little of its sparkle when there's no one to discuss it with afterwards. But just being with someone is no insurance against loneliness. The couples I meet aren't all soulmates. I hear bored, indifferent, and angry voices as I walk through a theater lobby.

You know all about loneliness, Jesus. So did Paul. I am trying, with some success, to make Paul's secret my own, to learn his knack for adjusting to any and all circumstances — by making You the focus of each day. Because you, Christ Jesus, are my Savior, I remind myself that I have Your strength within me. Weak though I am, I can do anything!

# 10 Facing Illness Alone

Who shall separate us from the love of Christ? Shall tribulation, or distress, or persecution, or famine, or nakedness, or peril, or sword? . . . No, in all these things we are more than conquerors through Him who loved us."

Romans 8:35, 37 RSV

God, I'm so afraid. I keep telling myself that I'll feel better soon, that this is just a temporary problem, and that all I need is a little rest. But what if it's more than that? What if something is seriously wrong?

Night after night I lie awake, imagining myself facing crushing medical expenses, surgery, pain, disability, even death – always alone. If only I had someone who would go with me to the doctor's office, someone to hold my hand. Sometimes I think there is no one who cares whether I live or die.

Yes, Lord. I know I'm exaggerating. The friends I care about surely feel the same way about me. But even so – there is no one whose life is bound up with mine, no one who really needs me, no one who would be willing to sacrifice self to take care of me.

No one but You. And deep in my heart, I know that You are all I really need. When I put my tomorrows into Your loving hands, I can make today count. I can cut my fears down to size by talking them over with You and with those who care about me. I can reject self-pity and choose to meet life with gratitude, humor, and faith.

Oh God, I know You are a Father who never forgets, who never turns His back. No matter how dark it seems, I believe that the love released by Your Son is at work in me right now. One step at a time, I — no, You and I — can and will conquer anything.

# 11 The Disappointment

We know that in all things God works for good with those who love Him, those whom He has called according to His purpose. . . . In view of all this, what can we say? If God is for us, who can be against us? Romans 8:28, 31 TEV

A door has shut. I must reshape my goals and abandon my rosy dreams for the future. They are fantasies that have no connection with reality.

It's not fair, Lord! How can You allow me to be cheated out of something that means so much to me? Why did You permit events beyond my control to limit my choices in this way? How can this crushing disappointment possibly work out for my good?

Now that I think about it, You didn't have all that many choices Yourself, did You? You put aside Your own needs and desires for the good of others — including me. You gave up prestige, home life, riches, power, comfort, even the loyalty of Your friends. You willingly carried out the Father's plan, at a cost far beyond my understanding.

Jesus, let this moment be a turning point in my life. Although I still don't see its meaning, help me accept Your decision. Keep me truly thankful for the other opportunities You have given me, instead of bemoaning the one that is gone. Let me cling to the love that You have promised and that will never leave me. Make Your work for good a reality in my life.

# 12 Friends

Jesus said to the servants, "Fill these jars with water." They filled them to the brim, and then He told them, "Now draw some water out and take it to the man in charge of the feast." They took him the water, which now had turned into wine, and he tasted it. He did not know where this wine had come from (but, of course, the servants who had drawn out the water knew); so he called the bridegroom and said to him, "Everyone else serves the best wine first, and after the guests have drunk a lot, he serves the ordinary wine. But you have kept the best wine until now!"

John 2:7-10 TEV

I feel so warm and happy inside tonight, nourished not only by a delicious dinner – but by the warm understanding, the wit, the stimulating conversation, the contagious faith, and the love of these very special friends.

You understand me so well, Lord Jesus. You built in me this need for fellowship, for communication, for sharing. You help me put aside my unreasonable fear of rejection and failure. Strengthened by Your love, I am more and more able to reach out to others with calm, casual friendliness – remembering that they also need to be wanted, accepted, and loved. Gently but firmly, You push me to be more open, more vulnerable, and more loving.

Then You bestow the wonderful, miraculous reward. A sterile, polite relationship blossoms into a vital, growing, and deeply rooted friendship.

In so many ways and on so many occasions, You turn water into wine.

# 13 Saturday Night

"I do not call you servants any longer, because a servant does not know what his master is doing. Instead, I call you friends, because I have told you everything I heard from My Father. You did not choose Me; I chose you and appointed you to go and bear much fruit, the kind of fruit that endures. And so the Father will give you whatever you ask of Him in My name. This, then, is what I command you: love one another.

John 15:15-17 TEV

Alone on Saturday night — again. The thing is, Lord, I don't fit in anywhere. Now that my old friends are all married, I'm not completely at ease with them anymore — and they seem less comfortable with me. Either they ask me to bring a date to their parties, or they insist on digging up an extra man for me. Why don't they just invite several singles, without this uncomfortable insistence on even numbers and possible pairs? Why don't they understand that most of the time I'd really rather come alone?

Yes, Lord. I know that's not fair. There's no way they can know how I feel unless I tell them. Give me tact enough to express my preferences without hurting anyone's feelings.

But what do I say to the "friend" who appears to see me as a threat to her marriage? I can't figure her out! Does she think I'll try to steal her husband away? Or does she envy the glamorously free life she imagines I lead?

Another thing. It's hard to believe, Lord, that it is

really concern for me that makes some old friends so inquisitive about the men in my life. They make such a big deal about any new and tentative friendship that I'm embarrassed to even speak to a man when they're around. If I try a new hairstyle or buy some new clothes, they immediately think that there's a new romance on my horizon. Even if it's true, what business is it of theirs?

Perhaps it's too much to expect old friendships to endure through the zigs and zags of life. Most — perhaps all — of Your disciples were new friends, weren't they, Jesus? The friends of Your boyhood stayed behind in Nazareth — and met You with hostility when You returned. You, too, experienced the pain of a friendship that withered away as two people grew in different directions. When habit is all that binds friends together and when we tear each other down instead of building up, perhaps it is time to say good-bye.

But that doesn't solve the problem of what to do on a Saturday night, does it? Help me remember, Lord, that neither old nor new relationships will survive unless I do my share of the weeding and the watering. Some of the time, I must be willing to put aside my preferences and adapt to someone else's plans. Some of the time, I must take the initiative and do the planning and telephoning — accepting the risk of rejection.

Let Your friendship so fill my life, Jesus, that it spills over to others. Lead me to those who need companionship as much as I. Relay Your message of love through me, rearranging my priorities so that I will have time for human relationships. Remind me daily of Your command to love.

Thank You, Lord, for being my unchanging Friend.

# 14 Worried

"Do not be anxious, saying, 'What shall we eat?' or 'What shall we drink?' or 'What shall we wear?' For the Gentiles seek all these things; and your heavenly Father knows that you need them all. But seek first His kingdom and His righteousness, and all these things shall be yours as well.

"Therefore do not be anxious about tomorrow, for tomorrow will be anxious for itself. Let the day's own trouble be sufficient for the day." Matthew 6:31-34 RSV

Whatever happened to reliability? honesty? integrity? Are such old-fashioned virtues now considered out of date? Everyone I meet has a horror story to tell — about repair shops that specialize in the runaround, builders who use shoddy materials, or workers who have no pride in what they do. New books expose one segment of society after another: greedy doctors, fraudulent advertisers, power-hungry politicians, and employers and employees who systematically cheat each other. "They're gonna get you," is the message, "unless you protect yourself or, better still, get them first."

Sometimes I feel very much alone in a hostile world. It just hit me, Lord: one day I will be *old.* And whether I am old and poor or old and comfortable depends almost entirely on me. I'm making more money than I ever dreamed possible — but spending it much faster than I want to — and probably being cheated out of some of it because I am too ignorant to defend myself.

Help me, Lord Jesus. I don't want to be victimized

by ripoff artists — but neither do I want to assume automatically that every person I meet is out to get me. Uphold me as I study investment options, automobile maintenance, and the pros and cons of home ownership. Help me tailor my interests and wants to fit my budget. Remind me to treat others as I would like to be treated, on the assumption that they are caring, honorable — but not infallible — people. Show me how to be realistically loving, that I may believe the best of people — but not tempt them unnecessarily.

Lord, I need Your protection, not only from the con artists but also from men who try too hard to help me. They mean well when they pat me on the head and say "Trust me" instead of giving straight answers to my questions. It's true that I wasn't brought up to think of money matters in my world, that was for men to do. Maybe I am a child in the world of finance — but, Lord, I resent being treated like one!

Strengthen me, O Lord, as I grow in my ability to make wise decisions. When I need advice, lead me to people who will treat me as a rational adult and help me to live up to that image. Let me be a good caretaker of all you have given me.

All these needs, Lord Jesus, are already known by Your Father and mine. Enable me to trust wholly in His loving care. Clear my mind of useless worry, and let Your Spirit focus my eyes on the concern I must rank above all others.

Your kingdom come, Lord — Your kingdom come.

# 15 Givers and Takers

Remember that the person who plants few seeds will have a small crop; the one who plants many seeds will have a large crop. Each one should give, then, as he has decided, not with regret or out of a sense of duty; for God loves the one who gives gladly. And God is able to give you more than you need, so that you will always have all you need for yourselves and more than enough for every good cause. 2 Corinthians 9:6-8 TEV

Why should I be the patsy, Lord? Good old dependable me! After all, I don't have a husband and children to look after. Obviously I am the logical person to handle the jobs no one else wants. When my parents need someone to stay with them for a while, everyone points at me. When my cousin from the country needs a job and place to live, they assure me that I'll have no trouble getting her into my office and that she'll be good company for me in my little apartment. When my nephew needs a down payment for a car, he looks to me because "I have no one else to spend my money on."

O God, I honestly do love them all – but I resent these one-sided relationships. Why do people accept all I give as their due – and take it for granted that it will continue indefinitely? I feel that they are taking advantage of me – and I don't like it one bit.

Forgive me, Lord. I am judging a whole group of people without any real understanding of their motives, fears, or feelings. Their behavior is their business, not mine. My job is to decide what role I want to play in life. Do I want to be a giver or a taker? There's no contest. You have given freely of Yourself to me and to others — I can attempt no less.

Make giving a way of life for me, Father, as it was for Your Son. Once I have made the basic commitment, help me plan where and to whom I will give — remembering that the neediest person is not necessarily the one who makes the most noise. Give this jellyfish backbone enough to say no when that is appropriate. Show me now to resist being stepped on — and still love.

Lord, when I share my time and money, show me where the real needs are; enable me to balance my obligations to self, family, friends, church, and community. Teach me to give with a whole heart, without counting the cost or expecting a return.

Heavenly Father, I know that every good thing in my life comes from You. Thank You for Your unstinting gifts.

Christ Jesus, I am in awe of Your love, Your sacrifice, Your emptying of Yourself. No matter how much I give, I can never match Your generosity to me.

Fill me, then, with Your abundant Spirit, that I may sow lavishly — and gather a harvest of joy everlasting.

# 16 Making a Difference

"Then the righteous will answer Him, 'Lord, when did we see Thee hungry and feed Thee, or thirsty and give Thee drink? And when did we see Thee a stranger and welcome Thee, or naked and clothe Thee? And when did we see Thee sick or in prison and visit Thee?' And the King will answer them, 'Truly, I say to you, as you did it to one of the least of these my brethren, you did it to Me.'" Matthew 25:37-40 RSV

Forgive me, Lord. How could I be so insensitive? How could I watch their agony and go right on eating? How could I forget that the figures in the TV newsclip are real, living, suffering people?

Lord, I don't mean to be cold and uncaring. But with instant communication all over the world, bereavement and hunger and cruelty have become commonplace. Bombarded as I am by tragic stories, I am compelled to put up my defenses. Without a detached viewpoint, I would tear myself apart.

The thing is, I feel so helpless. Overwhelming numbers of people, enormously complex problems – it's mind-boggling. How can one person make any impression on the vast sea of misery that covers the world?

Guide me, Lord Jesus, as I try to learn from the way You lived Your life here on earth. You healed many – but not all – of the sick in Israel. You fed large groups of people – but for only one meal. You washed dirty feet – but only those of Your disciples. Binding

Yourself to our limitations of time, space, and human endurance, You did what You could and left the rest to the Father.

Show me, Lord, how to do what I can where I can. Remind me that with Your unlimited power within me I can do more than now seems possible. If I cannot solve the problem of juvenile delinquency, I can offer faithful, caring friendship to one lonely child. No matter how depressing the poverty statistics, I can make a difference: I can teach one jobless adult to read or work at an inner city thrift shop or serve on a community task force. Out of thousands of lonely shut-ins, I can visit one regularly. Although I can't finance all the good things that need doing, I can recognize You as the Source of all I have—and give in proportion to my income. Enable me, Lord, to use insights from Your Word, advice from people I trust, and my own intelligence as I decide how to allocate the time and money I have set aside for You.

Open my eyes, O Christ, so that I may see Your face in those You want me to help each day. Let me never be too preoccupied with my daily routine to notice worried eyes or a trembling hand. Show me when and how to reach out to someone in trouble, how to offer help but never push it. Fill me with courage, eloquence, and a sure sense of timing as I seek to share my faith in You.

Lord Jesus, I put my whole life in Your hands. Allow me to live each day in the certainty of Your presence— but when the tragedies of this world make You seem far away, let me hang on to my faith and keep on working. Keep me always, imperfect though I am, a lighted pathway for Your love.

# 17 On My Birthday

"I have come in order that you might have life – life in all its fullness." John 10:10b TEV

I give up, Lord! In spite of my persistent prayers, I continue to be alone. I am invited to one wedding after another, but there is still no prospect of a wedding in my life. Each year, it is harder and harder to believe that soon I will find the someone who is right for me.

Don't get me wrong, Lord. I don't mean that I no longer want to be married. I honestly feel that I would be happiest in the traditional roles of wife and mother. But I accept Your verdict – marriage is not the gift You think appropriate for me, at least not now. Lovingly but firmly, You have said no to the barrage of specific prayers I have sent Your way.

So I submit my future to Your will – without any reservations. If Your gift for me is a single life, let it be so. Perhaps You have a special job in mind for me, something a single person can do best.

But I need your help, Jesus. You also led a single life; You understand the needs I have. When my feelings get too big for me to handle, I count on You to help me.

Show me how to use my aloneness to grow in independence – to enjoy solitude as well as companionship – to create an inviting home where I – and others – will find tranquillity, warmth, and renewal. Let me use my freedom to learn new skills, to find satisfying ways of working in Your vineyard, and to reach out to others who may be lonely, too. Teach me how to initiate and nourish friendship with both men and women.

I turn my life over to You, Lord Jesus. I trust completely in Your promise to bring me "life in all its fullness." Ready for surprises, I will follow (sometimes stumbling a little), wherever You lead.

# 18 My New Apartment

Miriam, Aaron's sister, took her tambourine, and all the women followed her, playing tambourines and dancing. Miriam sang for them:

"Sing to the Lord, because He has won
a glorious victory;
He has thrown the horses and their riders
into the sea."

Exodus 15:19-21 TEV

If I had a tambourine handy, I'd follow Miriam's example. You have bestowed many blessings on me, Lord, but this one is a real zinger! My own private, decorated-just-for-me apartment! Why didn't I take this step long ago?

Lord, You know why. Temporary living arrangements appeared best for a woman who expected marriage to be just around the corner. Any move toward settling down seemed a tacit admission that (shocking thought!) I might not marry at all. I even carted around cardboard boxes of assorted junk dating from my school days – with unspoken plans to sort it all out sometime soon – before I married. I gave all my energy to waiting instead of doing.

How stupid I was – as if leading an uncomfortably catch-as-catch-can life would somehow make me more attractive to a potential mate! When I finally analyzed my behavior, I realized that my kind of man would be far more interested in a self-sufficient woman who doesn't expect him to meet all her needs. And since I'm not willing to settle for a cheap substitute for the right marriage, I might as well build a fulfilling single lifestyle — which may indeed be permanent.

Lord God, my change of attitude is a victory as important (to me) as Miriam's. Thank You! Thank You for the pleasure I've found in dishes that match, in my secondhand shop finds, in the well-loved pieces from my childhood home, in one-of-a-kind creations I made myself. Guard me from the trap of allowing these newly cherished possessions to own me. Let me use them — and all Your gifts — in whatever service to which You call me, at each stage of my life.

For I have learned that each stage is good. Life keeps surprising me — but I am no longer afraid of surprises. Lord of Life, You have taught me to await each day with eager curiosity. What new blessing will You bring me today?

Father, let my new apartment be a symbol for me, a reminder that Your blessings have many disguises. They may look like confusion or pain or love or boredom or discovery or disappointment or delight — but, when received with thanks, each one is revealed as a unique gift from You. The circumstances that forced me to seek a new place to live were not of Your making — but Your creative power turned this crisis into a launching pad.

Lord, I'm off and running — maybe even dancing. Thank You! I rejoice in Your glorious victory!

# 19 Coming Home Alone

When I am ready to give up,
He knows what I should do.
In the path where I walk,
my enemies have hidden a trap for me.
When I look beside me,
I see that there is no one to help me,
no one to protect me.
No one cares for me.
Lord, I cry to You for help;
You, Lord, are my protector;
You are all I want in this life.
Listen to my cry for help,
for I am sunk in despair . . .
Set me free from my distress;
then in the assembly of Your people I will
praise You because of Your goodness to me.

Psalm 142:3-7 TEV – A Poem by David,
When He Was in the Cave

I dig in my bag for the key, turn it slo-o-owly in the lock, check my mailbox, and polish the doorknob with my sleeve. Sometimes I even volunteer to work late at the office – anything to put off going into that dark and silent apartment. Listening intently, I tell myself that the faint noises I hear inside are just the normal unexplained sounds of an empty place. Holding my breath, I quickly check each room, half-expecting someone to jump out at me.

Surely no believing Christian should have so little faith and so much fear! I am truly ashamed of my feelings,

Lord, and I ask Your forgiveness for them — but I have to admit that the pattern will probably repeat itself next time I come home alone. Thank You for loving and accepting me, fearful and foolish as I am.

Lord, You responded to David's cry for help. Be with me in the dark; protect me as You did David. Build my faith — and my common sense — that I may drive out unreasoning fear. If the unlikely happens and a crisis should come, help me to think quickly and act wisely. Remind me that each new situation brings with it a new call to do Your work.

With Your help, O God, David overcame his fear. He acted bravely and decisively, and people rallied to his support. Although he still faced many difficulties, he was not the deserted, helpless victim he had thought he was. I, too, can give intelligent thought to the hazards of living alone and plan appropriate safeguards. Perhaps I can banish fear by creating my own welcome — open the door to appetizing smells from a crockpot, or lights and music turned on by a timer.

Here and now, Lord, I turn over my fears to You, my Defender. Labor with me, that I may use my privacy and independence — and my fearfulness — for good. Show me the tasks You have for me each day.

Almighty God, surround me with Your strength and care. I praise You, now and always, for Your unceasing goodness to me!

# 20 Growing Pains

Fill your minds with those things that are good and that deserve praise; things that are true, noble, right, pure, lovely, and honorable. Put into practice what you learned and received from me, both from my words and from my actions. And the God who gives us peace will be with you.

Philippians 4:8-9 TEV

It hurts, Lord. It hurts to abandon my old ways of thinking, my old defenses. It's so much safer to back away, to avoid entanglement in other people's lives, to hang on to the past instead of making the most of today.

But something is happening inside me that compels a change! I used to think, Father, that I could earn Your love. Silly, wasn't it? Although I don't deserve Your love, I have it. Even when I turn my back on You, Your love awaits my return. All my life I have thought, "If I try a little harder, God will love me." Now I understand: *because* You love me, I can try a little harder to do Your will.

Paul was right. The direction of my life is set by the contents of my head—my picture of You, my image of myself, and my attitudes toward other people. When I look for the true and noble in this world, I notice beauty and goodness that I otherwise take for granted. I look into people's eyes instead of passing them by.

Heavenly Father, let Your vision of a good and beautiful creation transform my thinking—and my actions. And when I see the ugliness that sin has caused, show me also the good You have made. Your Son's love cut through the outer shells of tax-collectors, prostitutes, and thieves. Nourish that kind of love in my heart – that I, like Jesus, may be able to see through arrogance, hostility, and greed – able to reach the hurting, love-starved person underneath.

Whom am I kidding? The outwardly obnoxious, inwardly despairing person I know best is me! I need to remember that You, Lord, love me as I am. Then I can work to develop the potential that You have created within me.

Father, give me a clear mind as I figure out some optimistically realistic goals for the next few years. Push me to take positive steps to make those dreams come true. Teach me to choose growth instead of apathy, physical well-being instead of flab, service instead of self-indulgent laziness.

O God, You give peace. Thank You for this new day. Shield me from being overwhelmed by all my problems and all the areas in my life that need change. Walk with me as I live – and grow – one day at a time.

# 21 Mr. Right?

I pray that your love will keep on growing more and more, together with true knowledge and perfect judgment, so that you will be able to choose what is best.

Philippians 1:9 TEV

He's not the man my parents would have chosen for me, Lord. In fact, he's not at all like the idealized Mr. Right I used to dream about. But when we are together, none of that seems to matter. There's a lovely warm feeling of shared laughter, mutual understanding, and deep caring. The attraction I feel for him is a compelling, almost overpowering, force.

It's when I am alone that the doubt comes back. Uncomfortable questions push their way into my mind. Do I truly love him—or am I just tired of being alone? Could the two of us really build a good life together? On the other hand, isn't it a little ridiculous to refuse to settle for someone a little different from the mythical "perfect match"?

Forgive me, Lord Jesus. We both know that I am avoiding the real issue. Is it wrong for me to consider a life with someone who does not call You Lord? My hope is that someday he will find You—but what if it doesn't work out that way? Divided as we are, could he and I hope to build a united marriage? What would happen to my relationship with You? What about the children we might have?

It isn't that he's hostile to Your church, Lord. But

to him it's merely a social organization he's chosen not to join. And when I try to explain what You mean to me, my words get tangled up. Perhaps the words won't come because my thinking is fuzzy. I'm being forced to consider why I believe and act as I do, impelled to question ideas I have taken for granted all my life. Maybe I have been too complacent, too lazy, too willing to let my spiritual growth remain frozen at the level of age 13.

It's scary, Lord. I don't want to lose my faith – but at this point I'm not ready to give him up, either. Please focus Your light on my confused thoughts, my wavering faith. Let Your Spirit guide me to true knowledge, O Lord, as I study Your Word with new intensity. Lead me to other books and to people who will help me grow in love and good judgment. Stay close to me, Lord Jesus, as I struggle to choose what is best.

# 22 More than a Body

Have you forgotten that your body is the temple of the Holy Spirit, who lives in you, and is God's gift to you, and that you are not the owner of your own body? You have been bought, and at a price! Therefore bring glory to God in your body.
1 Corinthians 6:19-20 Phillips

Last night was a mistake, Lord — a bad one. For a little while I forgot — no, ignored — who I am as Your person. Searching impatiently for love and fulfillment, I found frustration and emptiness. I'm so ashamed.

In Jesus' name I ask Your forgiveness, Heavenly Father. You have forgiven me many times in the past; in many different ways I have failed to live in Your light. But this is the first time I have felt such revulsion for my own actions. Your Word tells me that Christ spoke much more sternly to the proud than to the weak. I know that Your Son died to set us free from all the chains that bind us. In spite of all this, Lord, I don't *feel* forgiven.

God, please help me! Give me confidence in Your promise of forgiveness. Convince me that my body is still good in Your sight. Help me remember that You accept every part of me. Remind me that You pour out Your love even when I am weak, indifferent, undeserving; You understand my feelings and desires, uncomfortable though they sometimes are.

Enable me, loving Father, to acknowledge those desires, realizing that I can decide not to satisfy them – and still be a whole person. Help me choose long-term fulfillment over instant gratification. Make my sexuality a positive, energy-giving force in my life. Remind me that I – and others – belong first of all to You.

Let Your Spirit always dwell within the imperfect temple of my body.

# 23 Intimacy

Jesus saw her weeping, and He saw how the people with her were weeping also; His heart was touched, and He was deeply moved . . . Jesus wept. John 11:33-35 TEV

My commandment is this: love one another, just as I love you. The greatest love a person can have for his friends is to give his life for them. And you are my friends if you do what I command you. John 15:12-14 TEV

You too, Lord. You were as human and as vulnerable as we are. You needed friends to share the bad times and the good times with you. You opened Your heart so completely that You weren't afraid to cry in front of Your friends.

I yearn for that openness, Lord Jesus. My feelings—joy, anger, worry—get painfully bottled up inside me. Prayer helps but I need someone to talk to—someone who will be there when I am happy and when I am hurting. What's wrong, Jesus? Why am I so alone? Has my search for friends become submerged in a quest for a one-and-only? Maybe. Whenever I meet someone new, I want him to be *the one.* In fact, I kid myself that he is—until the letdown. Meanwhile, I am too absorbed in him to have time for the other men and women I meet along the way—people who might fulfill some of my needs for closeness and sharing.

Forgive me, Lord Jesus, for looking at these friends of Yours from the perspective of *my* needs and *my* desires.

I have not valued them for themselves; I have forgotten that You considered each of us worth dying for. My emphasis has been on having a friend when I need one, not on being a friend when I am needed.

Bless my life with Your kind of friendship, Lord Jesus. Lead me to good companions, remembering that even You did not find perfect ones. Guide me as I weigh the qualities I consider truly important in a friend and help me to offer friendship worthy of that company. Since wit, integrity, and a loving spirit are inner qualities, remind me that first impressions are not terribly reliable.

Am I capable of intimacy? I don't know. But, Lord, I want to try! Teach me how to communicate openly—choosing the right person, the least threatening approach, and the opportune moment. Guard my tongue from babbling secrets that are not mine to tell. Give me Your ability to listen and to focus on the other person's point of view. Free me to touch and to show love in appropriate ways, always sensitive to the needs of others.

Lord Jesus, thank You for allowing me, unworthy though I am, to be one who calls you Friend. It seems almost unbelievable that You would have been willing to seal our friendship by dying for me—and yet You have assured me that this is so. Live in me and through me as You have promised, O dearest Friend, and teach me Your way of love.

# 24 The Mentor

Well, religion does make a person very rich, if he is satisfied with what he has. What did we bring into the world? Nothing! What can we take out of the world? Nothing! So then, if we have food and clothes, that should be enough for us. But those who want to get rich fall into temptation and are caught in the trap of many foolish and harmful desires, which pull them down to ruin and destruction. For the love of money is a source of all kinds of evil. Some have been so eager to have it that they have wandered away from the faith and have broken their hearts with many sorrows.

But you, man of God, avoid all these things. Strive for righteousness, godliness, faith, love, endurance, and gentleness.

1 Timothy 6:6-11 TEV

I don't know why I feel so guilty sometimes. There is *nothing* wrong with our relationship, Lord! True, he has become very important to me — and perhaps I am important to him. But there is no question of a sexual relationship between us, nothing his wife could possible object to — unless she believes the myth that all single women are predators, constantly on the prowl for a man.

This man is not my lover. He never will be. But our joint struggle on the job has forged an enduring friendship, a mutual respect. He is my advisor and teacher; I am his protégée, his disciple. He says he feels young again as he helps me learn the ropes of the profession we share.

Lord, he is necessary to me! A rookie just doesn't

get anywhere in this business without a sponsor, someone who understands where the opportunities are. It isn't as though I invented the relationship of apprentice/mentor. The most successful men I know all got their start in this way.

Father, Your all-seeing eye lays bare my every thought. I confess to You that I have had occasional brief feelings of attraction toward my friend. Unbidden, stupid, and sinful thoughts come into my mind — but I don't have to let them stay. Guard my thoughts, Lord God, that I may never by word or look convey such an idea to my colleague. Remind us both that the marriage bond is emotional as well as sexual. His commitment to his wife creates a barrier we dare not cross, a reserve that must not break down.

Thank You, Father, for the success my mentor has made possible for me. I enjoy being successful — the challenging job, good salary, and recognition. Would I give it all up tomorrow, if it interfered with my calling as a Christian? I hope so! Lord, keep my eyes firmly on my goal, that no temporary success may wean me from the real riches found only in You.

# 25 Time for a Change

See how much the Father has loved us! His love is so great that we are called God's children — and so, in fact, we are. This is why the world does not know us: it has not known God. My dear friends, we are now God's children, but it is not yet clear what we shall become. 1 John 3:1-2a TEV

I wonder sometimes whether I have a hidden reason for working long hours. I love my job (thank You, God!) but this is ridiculous. I don't have to drive myself to mind-numbing fatigue. Most of these tasks could just as well be delegated to others or not done at all. Has the *job* completely taken over my life?

Understandable, really. Here I am respected, admired, even feared a little. But out there? Most people seem to think I'm some kind of freak — a sexless, emotionless, hard-driving automaton grinding out money and success.

God, I realize I must accept some responsibility for this situation. For the past few years I have deliberately pushed aside my feminity, convinced (rightly or wrongly) that I must choose between being a success and being a woman. Professionally, I have accomplished more that I ever dreamed possible — but I'm wondering what I have missed. Is it too late to go back and reawaken that important but neglected part of me?

Not that I necessarily want to get married, Lord. Over the years, I've changed from a dewy-eyed dreamer waiting for my prince to a skeptical observer of other people's marriages. I don't see many good ones. True, I get a lump in my throat when I hold someone else's baby—but I accept the reality: motherhood is not for me.

It's time, though, to rethink my goals. Remind, Lord, that my place in Your family is far more important than any recognition from my peers could ever be. Although there's nothing wrong with professional success, it must never interfere with Your plans for me.

Lord God, show me how to become the person You intend me to be. Let me rediscover my emotions; release the tender and loving woman no one but You knows. Instill me with courage to reach out to other people and to risk rebuff or indifference. Give me your gentle compassion; let people in need take the place of the children I do not have. Make me a whole person who is unafraid to love and be loved.

Where do I begin? Where do I look for the new me? God, please hold my hand while I experiment. Maybe I'll look for a new apartment—or volunteer to be a Big Sister—or try a new hairstyle—or sign up for that class in racquetball—or plant tomatoes in a window box.

The courage to change must come from You—from Your steadfast, inexplicable love for me. Give me that courage, Lord, remembering that Your love will never change. Give me patience, remembering that change comes slowly. Give me faith for the times when I cannot see where You are leading me. If You, my loving Father, know the way, that's all I need.

# 26 Hometown Visit

"How is this possible?" the people exclaimed. "He's just a carpenter's son, and we know Mary His mother and His brothers—James, Joseph, Simon, and Judas. And His sisters—they all live here. How can He be so great?" And they became angry with Him!

Matthew 13:55-57a TLB

I wish everyone could get along without marrying, just as I do. But we are not all the same. God gives some the gift of a husband or wife, and others He gives the gift of being able to stay happily unmarried. So I say to those who aren't married, and to widows—better to stay unmarried if you can, just as I am.

1 Corinthians 7:7-8 TLB

Lord Jesus, I don't know whether to laugh or cry. Coming home was something I'd really looked forward to. I was eager to see all the people I used to know and—I admit it—I guess I wanted to show off a little. I thought they'd be impressed by the success I've found in my work and that they would rejoice in the respect I've earned from others in my profession. I thought they'd be proud of me.

But the only part of my life that interests them is whether or not I have a *man.* Who is he? Is he "serious" about me? When they learn that there is no special man in my life, their pity builds a wall between us. To them, it is incomprehensible that someone would choose to live alone.

It's true that sometimes I wish I had someone to take care of me—someone I could cling to when I feel frightened or lonely. But that's pure fantasy, a totally unrealistic picture of marriage. My life is a good one,

Lord Jesus — enriched with work that brings me fulfillment — spiced by freedom to serve You with large chunks of my time — blessed by loving friends. When trouble hits, You invite me to call on You for help — help that never fails to come.

I need Your affirmation now, Jesus. Keep me from reopening old wounds, reliving old mistakes, and reevaluating my life according to the standards of others. You understand how it feels to be put down by those who knew you as a child. Heal my foolish hurt feelings and restore my sense of humor.

Thank You for the special gift that is mine. Let me never doubt my value in Your eyes.

# 27 The Celibate

Love is as powerful as death;
  passion is as strong as death itself.
It bursts into flame
  and burns like a raging fire.
Water cannot put it out;
  no flood can drown it.
But if anyone tried to buy love with his wealth,
  contempt is all he would get.
Song of Songs 8:6b-7 TEV

Do you really expect me to resist that power, Lord? Do You think I can push aside the terrible yearning, the acute longing that I dare not express? Is a celibate life truly Your plan for me?

Lord, it's tough to be a celibate when society expects me to be a playgirl. Today's sexual freedom isn't free at all – it's almost mandatory. Too often, men seem to think that taking me to dinner entitles them to spend the night. Or perhaps they too feel society's pressure, feel a need to prove themselves. If both persons think the other expects a sexual relationship, is it surprising that they are tempted to exploit each other?

What am I saying? Of course I want sexual relationships, in the sense that my sexuality is an important part of who I am. But the sexuality You created in me is not limited to my body. It pervades everything I am and everything I do. It is part of my capacity for love, my ability to reach out to others, and my warm and human emotions. Because I am a sexual person, it is natural and right for me to be attracted to a man; it is good to form relationships within the limits You have established.

The confusing thing is that not everything agrees on what those limits are. Even my pastor refuses to tell me *exactly* what I should or should not do. That's frustrating, Lord — especially in a world that equates self-restraint with frigidity and warmth with sexual invitation. Fill me with Your vision of who I am, so that the world's labels will lose their power to confuse me. Give me the wisdom to make good decisions in the light of Your Word.

Thank You, Father, for Your good gift of sexuality. Make of my celibacy an opportunity to concentrate all my energies on You and Your will for me. As a whole person — body, mind, emotions, and spirit — let me remember that all I have and am and will be belongs to You.

# 28 Invisible at Church

"Where two or three are gathered in My name, there am I in the midst of them." Matthew 18:20 RSV

Ridiculous, isn't it? I'm here every Sunday for a while; then I get disgusted and stay away. No one appears to notice when I'm gone. No doubt they assume I'm off to some exotic place for a Swinging Singles weekend. Or perhaps they are waiting until I grow up and get married. It will be a long wait.

Forgive me, Lord. I suppose I am overreacting. Some kind people have done their best to include me in the life of this church. They invite me to come to Couples Club, Family Night, and Couples Bible Study, assuring me that those names aren't meant to exclude anyone. But somehow I feel like a poor relative. If the names don't mean what they say, why use them?

Lord, why can't they understand that we who don't fit the traditional family pattern have both special strengths and special needs? How can I help them see that all of us who are alone need to be accepted as we are right now? The never married, the divorced, the widowed – all are damaged by the unspoken assumption that in due time we will reorder our lives to fit the standard pattern of pairs. You worked with individuals, Lord Jesus. Why can't Your church do that, too?

Show me how to convince them, Lord, that singles are not incomplete, not failures. We have a lot to offer.

For instance, I know more about the realities of living alone than most people do. Surely some of the survival tactics I've learned would be useful to the newly widowed or divorced. Why doesn't the church do something to get us together?

I want some real work to do, a voice in decision-making, some genuine responsibility. Why do they make me feel like a visitor instead of part of the family? Why, Lord, is Your church so often a place where You Yourself might feel unwelcome?

I know, Lord. You love Your imperfect church and the stumbling humans in it. You are here with us as we worship and work together. We are all one in You. If the church needs changing, it isn't "they" who ought to make it happen, it's we. Beginning with me. Show me, Lord Jesus, where and how to begin.

# 29 A Feast for Today

What is life? To me, it is Christ.
Philippians 1:21a TEV

How fortunate I am to live in a time when a woman's identity need not depend on having a husband! A hundred years ago, I would have been an old maid aunt living with relatives, an unpaid servant working hard for room and board.

Things are different now. Lord Jesus, I rejoice in the freely chosen way of life You have allowed me, in the liberty and self-sufficiency that are mine. If I get into a rut, I have the power to cut my losses and get out, without consulting anyone else. I can change jobs, take a year's leave of absence to chase a dream, move across the country, and take on absorbing new commitments.

Funny — all that freedom to change makes me more contented with the life I now lead. Some people say I'm married to my job — and it does fill a very important need in my life. Other kinds of work might pay more, but by comparison they seem bland and sterile. When I think of how Your guidance has shaped my choices, my joy and gratitude overflows.

Pilot me, Lord, as the years ahead unfold. Sometimes I think that my future might include a man who would share my life — but I leave that up to You. Am I looking for a man? Maybe. But I'm not longing for one. Instead of yearning for what might be, I intend to feast on what You have given me today.

And when it comes right down to it, Lord, if all these gifts – my job, my independence, and my freedom – are stripped away, I will still be rich. I will still have You, my loving Savior. And to me as to St. Paul, life need contain only one essential. You, and You alone, are the substance of my life.

# 30 In Your Image

God created human beings, making them to be like Himself. He created them male and female.

Genesis 1:27 TEV

Israel, the Lord who created you says,
"Do not be afraid — I will save you.
I have called you by name — you are mine."

Isaiah 43:1 TEV

Keep telling me that I am Yours, Lord. I need to know that I am truly valuable in Your sight. Sometimes it seems as if there's no place in this city for someone like me.

In a Noah's ark society, it's almost a sin to be single. People ask, "Are you dating anyone interesting?" or "What? An attractive woman like you *not* married?" or, more bluntly, "Any prospects?" Because I am not one of a pair, they reason, there must be something wrong with me.

Lord, it's a struggle not to accept all these negative messages, hard to be sure I really am a worthwhile person. But You who created me are gloriously willing to claim me as Your own, to say that You see me as an important person. I need that affirmation, God: You have called me by name; I am truly Your beloved daughter.

I do believe this. Help me work through my unbelief.